GREEK MYTHOLOGY FOR TWEENS

A Young Adventurers Guide to Ancient Heroes, gods, and Legends

ISADORA LOUKANIS

GREEK MYTHOLOGY FOR TWEENS

A Young Adventurers Guide to Ancient
Heroes, gods, and Legends

ISADORA LOUKANIS

© Copyright 2024 - All rights reserved

It is not legal to reproduce, duplicate, or transmit any part of this document in either electronic means or in printed format. Recording of this publication is strictly prohibited.

Contents

Contents.. 4
Introduction... 6
Welcome to Ancient Greece!............................... 6
   How to Use This Book.. 10
Part 1... 15
The gods of Olympus... 15
Chapter 1.. 16
Meet the Olympians – The gods and Goddesses of Mount Olympus.. 16
Part 2... 32
Heroes and Monsters... 32
Chapter Two... 33
Perseus and the Gorgon – The Hero Who Defeated Medusa... 33
Chapter Three... 46
Theseus and the Minotaur – The Labyrinth and the Monster... 46
Chapter Four.. 60
Hercules – The 12 Labors of the World's Strongest Hero.. 60
Chapter Five... 72
The Mythical Creatures of Ancient Greece........... 72
Part 3... 83
Epic Quests and Legendary Adventures................ 83
Chapter Six... 84
Jason and the Argonauts – The Quest for the Golden Fleece.. 84

Chapter Seven	94
Odysseus – The Epic Journey of the Odyssey	94
Part 4	105
The Underworld and the gods of Death	105
Chapter Eight	106
Hades, Persephone, and the Underworld	106
Chapter Nine	118
Orpheus and Eurydice – A Love Story from the Underworld	118
Part 5	127
Learning from Myths – Lessons for Life	127
Chapter Ten	128
What Greek Myths Teach Us About Friendship, Bravery, and Curiosity	128
Glossary of Mythological Terms	138
Conclusion	144

Introduction

Welcome to Ancient Greece!

Welcome, young adventurer! Have you ever wondered what it would be like to live in a world where gods and goddesses rule the skies, seas, and even the underworld? A world where brave heroes set out on dangerous quests to battle monsters, and where magical creatures hide in forests and caves? Well, you're about to find out!

In this book, you'll step into the magical world of **Ancient Greece**, a place where myths and legends come to life. Greek mythology is full of incredible stories about powerful gods like **Zeus**, the king of the gods, and **Athena**, the goddess of wisdom and war. These gods aren't just sitting on clouds—they're busy influencing everything from the weather to wars, and sometimes they even come down to earth to get involved in human affairs. But that's not all! You'll also meet **heroes** like **Hercules**, who fought a lion with his bare hands, and **Perseus**, who defeated the terrifying **Medusa**.

The world of Greek mythology is an exciting place where anything can happen. Imagine riding on **Pegasus**, a flying horse, or outsmarting a tricky **Sphinx** with its riddles. Every story is an adventure, filled with danger, mystery, and excitement. And the best part? You get to come along for the ride!

What is Greek Mythology?

Greek mythology is like a magical storybook passed down through generations. The ancient Greeks told these stories to explain the world around them. Imagine living thousands of years ago, before modern science and technology existed. If there was a lightning storm, instead of thinking about weather patterns, the Greeks would say that **Zeus** was angry and throwing his thunderbolts! If the seas were rough, it was because **Poseidon**, the god of the sea, was stirring the waters.

But Greek mythology isn't just about gods and goddesses. It's also about **heroes**—ordinary people who did extraordinary things. Heroes like **Theseus**, who bravely fought the **Minotaur** in a labyrinth, and **Jason**, who led a crew of the bravest warriors on a quest for the **Golden Fleece**. These heroes weren't perfect; they had flaws, made mistakes, and faced impossible challenges. But they always found a way to rise above and become legends.

You'll also meet **monsters**—some of the most imaginative and terrifying creatures ever imagined! There's the **Hydra**, a serpent with multiple heads, and **Cerberus**, the giant three-headed dog who guards the gates of the Underworld. These creatures are powerful, but don't worry—there are always heroes brave enough to take them on.

Greek mythology was an important part of life in ancient Greece. These stories helped the Greeks understand big ideas like love, death, nature, and the universe. They also served as lessons, teaching people how to be brave, smart, and kind. Even today, these myths inspire books, movies, and art, reminding us that these ancient stories still have something to teach.

How to Use This Book

Now that you've stepped into the world of Greek mythology, get ready for an unforgettable journey! This book is your guide to some of the most famous (and some not-so-famous) stories from ancient

Greece. Here's how it's organized to help you on your adventure:

- **Discover the gods and Goddesses**: In the first part of the book, you'll meet the most powerful gods and goddesses who live on Mount Olympus. You'll learn about their powers, their stories, and even their arguments (because, believe it or not, the gods didn't always get along!). Whether it's Zeus controlling the sky or Athena teaching heroes how to outsmart their enemies, each god and goddess has a role to play in the world of myths.
- **Heroes and Their Amazing Adventures**: Next, we'll dive into the action-packed adventures of some of the greatest heroes in Greek mythology. Theseus, Perseus, Hercules—each hero had their own quest, filled with danger and excitement. But don't

worry, you'll get to see how they used their strength, courage, and cleverness to overcome even the toughest challenges. And you might be surprised by what you can learn from them!

- **Creatures of Legend**: Greek myths aren't just about gods and heroes—they're also about the wild and wondrous creatures that roamed the ancient world. From the terrifying **Gorgons** to the mischievous **Satyrs**, each creature has its own story and its own lesson to teach. Some are scary, some are funny, but all of them will spark your imagination.
- **Adventures and Life Lessons**: Every chapter has a special adventure for you to follow, but that's not all. After each story, we'll explore the lessons that we can learn from these myths. Whether it's about **friendship, bravery,** or **facing fears**, there's always something to take away. Think of it as

a secret message hidden in every story, just waiting for you to discover.

- **Fun Facts and Surprising Details**: Throughout the book, you'll find fun facts about ancient Greece, its culture, and how these myths were passed down through generations. You'll also see how the stories of Greek mythology have influenced modern life—from movies and books to popular sayings and even brand names!

As you read, don't be afraid to let your imagination run wild. Picture yourself alongside Hercules as he battles a monster or flying through the sky with Pegasus. Each story is a gateway to a world where anything is possible, and YOU are the adventurer exploring it all.

By the end of the book, you'll be an expert in Greek mythology. You'll know all about the gods, the heroes, and the creatures that made these stories unforgettable. And who knows? Maybe you'll even be inspired to write your own myth!

Part 1

The gods of Olympus

Chapter 1

Meet the Olympians – The gods and Goddesses of Mount Olympus

Welcome to Mount Olympus! In this chapter, we're going to meet the mighty gods and goddesses who ruled from the top of this magnificent mountain. These aren't just any gods—these are the **Olympians**, the most powerful beings in Greek mythology. They controlled everything: the sky, the seas, the earth, and even the lives of mortals. From Zeus, the king of the gods, to Poseidon, the ruler of the seas, these deities had incredible powers, and their stories are as exciting as any adventure you can imagine!

Let's start with the king himself, **Zeus**, and then work our way through his family and fellow Olympians.

Zeus, the King of the gods

Zeus wasn't just any god—he was the **boss** of all the gods and goddesses. With his mighty **thunderbolt** in hand, Zeus ruled from the top of **Mount Olympus**, keeping the other gods in line and making sure the universe ran smoothly. He wasn't just the god of the sky, he also controlled the weather, bringing rain, storms, and sunshine as he pleased. In many ways, Zeus was like a superhero, but he also had a temper that could shake the world.

Zeus's Thunderbolt and His Adventures

Have you ever heard thunder during a storm? According to Greek mythology, that's the sound of **Zeus** throwing his mighty thunderbolt! Zeus's thunderbolt was his most powerful weapon, and with just one throw, he could defeat giants, monsters, and anyone who dared to challenge him.

But Zeus wasn't just all about power—he was also known for his many adventures and battles to protect the gods and mortals from danger. One of his most famous adventures was his battle against the

Titans. Before the Olympians ruled, the Titans were the rulers of the universe. They were enormous and powerful, but Zeus, along with his brothers **Poseidon** and **Hades**, led the Olympians in a war to overthrow the Titans. After a fierce battle, Zeus won and became the king of the gods.

Impact on gods and Mortals:

As king, Zeus kept an eye on everything happening in the world. He watched over mortals (humans) and made sure that justice was served. If someone was cruel or dishonest, Zeus would send a thunderbolt to remind them who's in charge. But he was also a protector, helping mortals when they were in trouble and making sure that the gods didn't interfere too much in human lives.

Hera, Queen of the gods

Right by Zeus's side was his wife, **Hera**, the **queen of the gods**. While Zeus ruled the skies, Hera was the protector of **marriage** and **families**. She was a powerful and majestic goddess, and although she sometimes had disagreements with Zeus (which is understandable, since Zeus could be a bit mischievous), Hera was fiercely protective of her family and the other gods.

Hera's Strength and Devotion

Hera was known for her incredible strength, not just in terms of power, but also in her **loyalty** and **devotion** to those she cared about. Even though Zeus wasn't always the most faithful husband, Hera never stopped protecting her family. She watched over marriages on Earth, blessing those who honored love and commitment.

One famous story about Hera's strength comes from the time when she and the other gods rebelled against Zeus. They were upset with his bossy ways and decided to overthrow him. Hera was the mastermind behind the plan, showing her strategic thinking and courage. Although their plan didn't work out (Zeus escaped and took back his throne), Hera's boldness showed that she wasn't afraid to stand up for herself and what she believed in.

Impact on Mortals:

Hera played a big role in the lives of mortals, especially when it came to protecting women and children. She was seen as a guardian of marriage, and many women prayed to her for a happy and strong family. If someone disrespected marriage, though, Hera wasn't afraid to punish them—just like Zeus used his thunderbolt, Hera used her own powers to make sure people respected the values she held dear.

Athena, Goddess of Wisdom and War

Have you ever faced a tough challenge and thought about using your brainpower to solve it? That's exactly what **Athena**, the **goddess of wisdom and war**, is all about. Athena wasn't just a warrior—she was the smartest of the gods, known for her incredible **wisdom**, **strategy**, and **fairness**. She preferred using her intelligence to solve problems rather than just fighting her way out.

The Birth of Athena

Athena has one of the most unusual birth stories in mythology. She wasn't born in a typical way—instead, she sprang fully grown and armored out of **Zeus's head**! Here's how it happened: Zeus had a headache, and it turned out to be a little more serious than your average headache! Hephaestus, the god of the forge, cracked Zeus's head open with an axe, and out came Athena, fully dressed in her armor, ready to fight and defend her people.

Athena and Heroes

Athena was a friend to many heroes, especially those who used their brains as well as their strength. One of her most famous partnerships was with **Perseus**, the hero who defeated **Medusa**, a monster with snakes for hair. Athena gave Perseus the tools he needed to win—like a shiny shield he used to avoid Medusa's deadly gaze by looking at her reflection instead of directly at her.

Impact on Mortals:

As the goddess of wisdom, Athena helped mortals with anything related to **intelligence** and **craftsmanship**. She was the goddess people prayed to when they needed to come up with a smart solution to a tough problem. Athena also taught mortals important skills, like weaving and pottery, which were valuable in ancient Greece.

Apollo, God of Music, Prophecy, and Healing

Meet **Apollo**, the **god of music**, **prophecy**, and **healing**. Apollo was known for his bright and radiant energy, just like the **sun**. In fact, one of his jobs was to ride his golden chariot across the sky each day, bringing light and warmth to the world. But Apollo was also much more than a sun god—he was a master of the arts and a skilled healer.

Apollo and the Arts

Apollo loved all kinds of music and art. He played the **lyre**, a beautiful instrument that sounded like magic, and wherever Apollo went, music followed. He inspired artists, musicians, and poets to create masterpieces, and he held contests to see who could create the most beautiful music.

Apollo and the Oracle of Delphi

One of Apollo's most important roles was as the god of **prophecy**. People came from all over Greece to visit the **Oracle of Delphi**, a sacred place where Apollo would share his wisdom and predictions about the future. The oracle was believed to be able to tell people their destiny, thanks to Apollo's guidance.

Apollo, the Healer

In addition to his artistic talents, Apollo was also a **healer**. If someone was sick or injured, they would pray to Apollo for help. His knowledge of medicine allowed him to heal people and save lives.

Impact on Mortals:
Apollo was beloved by artists, musicians, and anyone who sought wisdom about the future. People visited his temples to seek guidance about their lives, and many believed that Apollo's music could heal not just their bodies, but also their hearts.

Artemis, Goddess of the Hunt and Nature

If you love animals and exploring the great outdoors, then you'll love **Artemis**, the **goddess of the hunt and nature**. Artemis was Apollo's twin sister, and while he was all about music and light, Artemis was wild and free, ruling over the forests and protecting the creatures that lived there.

Artemis's Wilderness Adventures

Artemis was a skilled hunter, and she spent most of her time roaming the forests, bow in hand, accompanied by her loyal band of nymphs (young goddesses of nature). She was known for her incredible aim and her love of nature. But Artemis wasn't just about hunting—she was also a protector of young girls and animals, making sure they were safe from harm.

One of Artemis's most famous adventures involved the **Calydonian Boar**, a monstrous creature that terrorized the land. Artemis was called upon to help, and with her unmatched hunting skills, she played a key role in defeating the beast.

Impact on Mortals:
People looked to Artemis for protection, especially young girls and women. She was a symbol of independence, strength, and loyalty to those she loved.

Poseidon, God of the Sea

Next, let's dive into the realm of **Poseidon**, the **god of the sea**. With his powerful **trident**, Poseidon ruled over all the oceans, rivers, and lakes. His temper was as wild as the sea itself—when he was happy, the waters were calm, but when he was angry, he stirred up terrible storms and earthquakes.

Poseidon's Control Over the Seas

Poseidon's power over the sea meant that sailors and fishermen prayed to him for safe travels and good fortune. He could calm the waves or whip them into a frenzy. One famous story of Poseidon's power involves his rivalry with **Athena** over who would be the protector of the city of **Athens**. To impress the people, Poseidon struck the ground with his trident and created a saltwater spring, but Athena offered them the olive tree, a symbol of peace and prosperity. The people chose Athena, and Poseidon wasn't too happy about it!

Poseidon's Temper

Poseidon's temper was legendary. If someone disrespected him, he would send massive waves or even earthquakes to remind them of his power. But despite his temper, Poseidon was also a protector of sailors and fishermen who honored him.

Impact on Mortals:
Sailors, fishermen, and anyone who traveled by sea

prayed to Poseidon for safe journeys. He was both feared and respected, and many temples were built in his honor along the coasts of Greece.

Other Olympians: Hermes, Demeter, Ares, Aphrodite, and Hephaestus

While Zeus, Hera, Athena, Apollo, Artemis, and Poseidon are some of the most well-known Olympians, there were other gods and goddesses who played important roles in the lives of both mortals and other gods.

- **Hermes**, the **messenger god**, was known for his speed and cleverness. He carried messages between the gods and mortals, wearing his famous winged sandals.
- **Demeter**, the **goddess of agriculture**, was responsible for the harvest and the changing seasons. Her story with her daughter Persephone explains why we have winter and summer.
- **Ares**, the **god of war**, loved battle and chaos. He represented the more violent side of war,

unlike his sister Athena, who represented strategic warfare.
- **Aphrodite**, the **goddess of love and beauty**, was said to be the most beautiful of all the goddesses. She had the power to make anyone fall in love.
- **Hephaestus**, the **god of fire and the forge**, was the blacksmith of the gods, creating their weapons and tools. Even though he wasn't as physically strong as the other gods, he was incredibly talented and valued for his skills.

Each of these Olympians had their own special powers and stories, making the world of Greek mythology even richer and more fascinating.

Interactive Element: Create Your Own Olympian

Now that you've met the Olympians, it's time to use your imagination! If you were a god or goddess living on Mount Olympus, what would your special power be? Would you control the weather like Zeus, or protect animals like Artemis? Maybe you'd be the god of sports or the goddess of technology!

Think about these questions:

- What would your name be?
- What powers would you have?
- What would you wear? (Remember, gods and goddesses love cool outfits!)
- What responsibilities would you have? Would you help mortals or cause mischief?

Take some time to draw or describe your own Olympian. Be creative—you're part of the adventure now!

That's the end of our first chapter! We've met the powerful Olympians and learned about their incredible stories. In the next chapter, we'll dive into the adventures of some of the greatest heroes in Greek mythology.

Part 2

Heroes and Monsters

Chapter Two

Perseus and the Gorgon – The Hero Who Defeated Medusa

Welcome to one of the most thrilling adventures in all of Greek mythology—the story of **Perseus** and **Medusa**. In this chapter, we're going to follow Perseus on his incredible quest to defeat Medusa, a terrifying creature with snakes for hair and a gaze that could turn anyone into stone. This is no ordinary tale—Perseus doesn't just rely on his strength; he uses his **cleverness**, help from the gods, and some magical tools to complete his mission.

Let's jump right into the adventure!

The Quest for Medusa's Head

Our story begins on the island of **Seriphus**, where Perseus lived with his mother, **Danaë**. Their lives were peaceful until the island's king, **Polydectes**, became obsessed with Danaë and wanted to marry her. However, Danaë did not return his feelings, and Polydectes saw Perseus as an obstacle. To get rid of him, the king came up with a dangerous challenge that he was sure would lead to Perseus's doom. He told Perseus that he wanted the head of **Medusa**, one of the three monstrous sisters known as the **Gorgons**, as a wedding gift. Medusa was infamous for her ability to turn anyone who looked at her into stone, making her a deadly opponent.

Polydectes thought Perseus would never survive such an impossible task, but Perseus was not one to back down. He bravely accepted the challenge, even though he knew it would be incredibly dangerous. But Perseus had something on his side that Polydectes didn't count on—he had the **gods** watching over him.

Help from the gods: Athena and Hermes

Before Perseus set out on his quest, the gods **Athena** and **Hermes** decided to help him. After all, no hero could defeat a monster like Medusa alone!

Athena, the **goddess of wisdom and war**, gave Perseus a **bronze shield** that was polished so perfectly it acted like a mirror. She told him, "**Do not look directly at Medusa, for her gaze will turn you to stone. Instead, look at her reflection in this shield.**" Perseus knew this was key to his success.

Next, **Hermes**, the **messenger god**, arrived to give Perseus a **special sword**. This wasn't just any sword—it was sharp enough to slice through even the hardest scales, like those of Medusa. Hermes also gave Perseus a pair of **winged sandals** that would allow him to fly, helping him travel quickly and escape danger when needed.

But there was still more Perseus needed. To find Medusa, Perseus had to locate the **Nymphs of the North**, who had more magical items for him. Hermes told him how to reach them, and with his winged sandals, Perseus flew swiftly to their hidden land.

When Perseus arrived, the Nymphs gave him three more gifts: a **magic wallet** to carry Medusa's head, a **helmet of invisibility** (which belonged to Hades, the god of the underworld), and **directions to Medusa's lair**.

Now armed with Athena's shield, Hermes's sword and sandals, and the magical items from the Nymphs, Perseus was ready to face Medusa.

Medusa's Backstory

Before we get to Perseus's encounter with Medusa, let's learn a little more about this fearsome creature.

36

Medusa wasn't always a monster—in fact, she was once a beautiful woman with long, flowing hair. But her life took a dark turn when she angered the goddess **Athena**.

The story goes that Medusa was a priestess in one of Athena's temples. She was known for her beauty, but instead of keeping her vows to Athena, Medusa allowed the sea god **Poseidon** to court her. This made Athena furious, and as punishment, she transformed Medusa into a hideous monster. Medusa's beautiful hair became a writhing mass of **snakes**, and anyone who looked directly at her was instantly turned into **stone**.

To make matters worse, Medusa wasn't just an ordinary monster—she was a **Gorgon**, one of three terrifying sisters. Her sisters, **Stheno** and **Euryale**, were also fearsome, but Medusa was the only one who was mortal, which meant she could be killed. Despite her fearsome abilities, Medusa lived in hiding, away from both gods and mortals, in a gloomy cave surrounded by statues—people who had made the fatal mistake of looking at her.

Perseus's Encounter with Medusa

Armed with the knowledge of Medusa's powers and the gifts from the gods, Perseus set out on his final journey. Flying with his winged sandals, he soon reached the lair of the **Gorgons**, a place filled with statues of those who had tried and failed to defeat Medusa.

Perseus knew this was the moment of truth. He crept quietly into the cave, careful not to look directly at Medusa. Remembering Athena's advice, he used the **reflective shield** to safely navigate the dark, eerie cave. In the mirror-like surface, he could see Medusa sleeping. Her snaky hair twisted and coiled, but she was unaware of Perseus's presence.

With one swift motion, Perseus raised the sword that Hermes had given him and, without looking directly at Medusa, struck her head off in one clean blow! As her head separated from her body, Medusa's **snakes** hissed one last time, and her body slumped to the ground. Perseus quickly placed her head into the **magic wallet** given to him by the Nymphs, careful not to look at it.

But Perseus wasn't out of danger yet! Medusa's sisters, Stheno and Euryale, woke up and, filled with rage, chased after Perseus. Fortunately, Perseus had one more magical trick up his sleeve—the **helmet of invisibility**. As soon as he put it on, he vanished from sight, escaping the furious Gorgons without a trace.

The Journey Home

With Medusa's head safely hidden in the magic wallet, Perseus began his journey back to Seriphus. But even after defeating one of the deadliest creatures in Greek mythology, Perseus's adventures weren't over.

As Perseus flew over the sea, he spotted a young woman chained to a rock, with a massive sea monster, called a **Kraken**, approaching her. This woman was **Andromeda**, the daughter of the king and queen of **Ethiopia**. Andromeda had been offered as a sacrifice to the Kraken because her mother had insulted the gods by claiming she was more beautiful than the **Nereids**, the sea nymphs.

Perseus, being the brave hero that he was, couldn't just fly by without helping. He swooped down to the rock and spoke to Andromeda, asking her who she was and why she was tied up. Learning of her plight, Perseus made a deal with Andromeda's father—the king. If Perseus could defeat the Kraken and save Andromeda, he would be allowed to marry her.

As the Kraken approached, Perseus pulled Medusa's head from his bag, careful not to look at it himself. The moment the Kraken caught sight of Medusa's face, it turned into solid **stone**, sinking beneath the waves, never to trouble Andromeda or her people again.

Andromeda was saved, and true to his word, the king agreed to let Perseus marry her. Together, they returned to Seriphus, where Perseus had unfinished business with **King Polydectes**.

Perseus's Return to Seriphus

When Perseus finally returned to Seriphus, he discovered that Polydectes had continued to harass his mother, Danaë. This enraged Perseus, and he marched straight to the king's palace.

Polydectes laughed when he saw Perseus, thinking the young hero had failed in his impossible task. But Perseus had the ultimate weapon with him—Medusa's head. As Polydectes and his court mocked him, Perseus calmly reached into his bag and pulled out the **severed head of Medusa**.

Before anyone had time to react, Polydectes and his entire court turned to stone, forever frozen in place. With the evil king defeated, Perseus placed the head back in his bag and freed his mother from the king's tyranny.

Afterward, Perseus returned the magical items to the gods who had lent them to him, and he and Andromeda went on to live a peaceful and happy life.

What We Learn from Perseus

Perseus's journey wasn't just about defeating a monster—it's a story filled with valuable lessons that we can all learn from. Let's break down some of the key lessons from Perseus's adventure:

1. Bravery in the Face of Danger

One of the most important lessons we learn from Perseus is the value of **bravery**. Even though his task seemed impossible, Perseus didn't back down. He knew that facing Medusa would be dangerous, but he accepted the challenge with courage and determination. In life, we all face challenges that seem scary or overwhelming, but Perseus shows us that we can conquer our fears if we stay brave and focused.

2. Using Your Intelligence and Resources

Perseus didn't defeat Medusa by brute strength alone—he used his **intelligence** and the **tools** given to him by the gods. The reflective shield from Athena, the winged sandals from Hermes, and the helmet of invisibility all played a critical role in helping Perseus succeed. This teaches us that being smart and using the resources available to us is just as important as being strong.

3. Never Giving Up, Even When Things Seem Impossible

From the beginning, Perseus's quest seemed impossible. But instead of giving up, Perseus pressed forward, no matter how difficult the task. This is a powerful reminder that even when things seem hopeless, we should keep pushing toward our goals. Perseus shows us the value of perseverance and never giving up, no matter how big the challenge may seem.

4. Helping Others Along the Way

Even though Perseus's mission was to defeat Medusa, he didn't hesitate to help others when he saw them in need—like when he rescued Andromeda from the Kraken. Perseus's actions remind us that, while it's important to focus on our own goals, it's also important to help others whenever we can.

Conclusion: A Hero for the Ages

Perseus's adventure is one of the most famous and exciting stories in Greek mythology. His journey teaches us about bravery, cleverness, and never giving up in the face of danger. With the help of the gods and his own determination, Perseus was able to accomplish the impossible and become a hero for the ages.

In the next chapter, we'll dive into another epic adventure with a new hero and a new set of challenges. But for now, take a moment to think about Perseus's story and the lessons we can take from it. What challenges are you facing in your life, and how can you use your bravery and intelligence to overcome them?

Chapter Three

Theseus and the Minotaur – The Labyrinth and the Monster

Get ready, young adventurer, because this chapter is all about bravery, cunning, and a terrifying beast called the **Minotaur**. Our hero, **Theseus**, is about to embark on one of the greatest adventures in all of Greek mythology—a journey deep into a twisting labyrinth, where a monster with the body of a man and the head of a bull lurks, ready to devour anyone who dares to enter.

But Theseus is no ordinary hero. He's smart, courageous, and willing to risk everything to protect his people. Let's dive into this epic tale and see how Theseus uses both his strength and his intelligence to defeat one of the most dangerous creatures in ancient Greece.

The Maze and the Beast

Our story begins in the great city of **Athens**, where Theseus was raised by his father, **King Aegeus**. Life in Athens was peaceful for the most part, but across the sea, there was a powerful kingdom called **Crete**, ruled by the cruel and cunning King **Minos**.

Minos had a dark secret—he kept a monstrous creature called the **Minotaur** hidden in a gigantic maze known as the **Labyrinth**. The Minotaur was half-man, half-bull, and completely terrifying. It lived only to kill and eat anyone who was unfortunate enough to be thrown into the maze.

But why did King Minos keep such a terrible monster? The story goes that Athens had once been at war with Crete and, after losing, had to agree to a terrible deal: every nine years, the Athenians had to send **seven boys and seven girls** to Crete as a **tribute**. These young Athenians were sent into the Labyrinth, where they would become food for the Minotaur. It was a punishment that filled the people of Athens with fear and sadness.

Theseus Steps Forward

As the time for the next tribute drew near, the people of Athens were heartbroken, knowing that fourteen of their young citizens would soon be sacrificed to the Minotaur. But this time, **Theseus**—brave, bold, and determined to protect his people—stepped forward.

"I will go," Theseus declared. "I will enter the Labyrinth and slay the Minotaur, freeing Athens from this terrible curse!"

The people of Athens were shocked. How could anyone, even a hero as strong as Theseus, survive the **Labyrinth**? It was a maze so complicated that once you entered, there was no way out. Even if Theseus managed to defeat the Minotaur, he would never be able to find his way back.

But Theseus was determined. He sailed to Crete with the other young Athenians, ready to face the terrifying monster.

Ariadne's Help

When Theseus and the other Athenians arrived in Crete, they were brought before **King Minos**. The king looked at Theseus and smirked. "So, you think you can defeat my Minotaur?" he said mockingly. "Many have tried, and all have failed. You will never leave the Labyrinth alive."

Theseus, undeterred by the king's words, replied, "We'll see about that."

But it wasn't King Minos who caught Theseus's attention—it was **Ariadne**, the king's daughter. Ariadne had heard about Theseus's bravery and, unlike her father, she had a kind heart. She didn't want to see Theseus or the other Athenians perish in the Labyrinth.

That night, Ariadne secretly approached Theseus. "I want to help you," she whispered. "I know how to defeat the Minotaur, and I can help you find your way out of the Labyrinth."

Theseus, surprised by her kindness, listened carefully. Ariadne handed him a **ball of thread**.

"When you enter the Labyrinth, tie one end of this thread to the entrance," she explained. "As you move deeper into the maze, unwind the thread behind you. Once you've defeated the Minotaur, you can follow the thread back to the entrance."

Theseus smiled, realizing that Ariadne's plan was brilliant. "Thank you, Ariadne," he said. "I promise that I will defeat the Minotaur and return."

Entering the Labyrinth

The next morning, Theseus and the other young Athenians were led to the entrance of the **Labyrinth**. The walls of the maze were tall and twisted, stretching out in every direction. It was clear that without Ariadne's help, Theseus would never find his way out once he entered.

As he stood at the entrance, Theseus tied one end of the thread to a rock and began to unwind it as he ventured into the dark and eerie maze. The walls seemed to close in around him, and the winding paths made it easy to lose his sense of direction. But Theseus remained focused, following the path deeper and deeper into the heart of the Labyrinth.

The silence was unsettling. Every step he took echoed through the maze, and Theseus knew that the **Minotaur** could be lurking around any corner.

Finally, after what felt like hours of wandering, Theseus heard a low, rumbling growl. His heart raced as he realized he was getting closer to the Minotaur's lair.

Suddenly, the Minotaur appeared—a towering beast with the body of a man and the head of a bull. Its eyes glowed with fury, and its sharp horns gleamed in the dim light. It snorted angrily, charging at Theseus with terrifying speed.

52

Theseus's Battle with the Minotaur

Theseus knew that this would be the most dangerous fight of his life. But he wasn't afraid. He had trained for this moment, and he knew that his strength and skill would help him defeat the monster.

As the Minotaur charged, Theseus quickly dodged out of the way, grabbing a nearby stone from the ground and hurling it at the beast. The Minotaur roared in anger, but the blow barely slowed it down. It charged again, its horns aiming for Theseus.

This time, Theseus was ready. With lightning-fast reflexes, he grabbed the Minotaur by its horns and twisted its massive head, forcing the creature to the ground. The Minotaur thrashed wildly, but Theseus held on, using all his strength to overpower the beast.

Finally, with one swift motion, Theseus drew his sword and struck the Minotaur down. The creature let out one final roar before collapsing to the ground, defeated.

Theseus stood over the Minotaur, breathing heavily. The battle had been fierce, but he had triumphed. The Minotaur was dead, and the people of Athens were free from their terrible curse.

But now, Theseus faced a new challenge—finding his way out of the Labyrinth. Thankfully, he still had the **thread** that Ariadne had given him. Following the string, Theseus retraced his steps, winding his way back through the twisting maze. After what seemed like an eternity, he finally saw the light of the entrance ahead.

Theseus emerged from the Labyrinth, victorious, with the other young Athenians following behind him. They were free, and the Minotaur was no more.

Ariadne's Escape Plan

When Theseus returned to the palace, Ariadne was waiting for him, her face filled with hope and worry. When she saw Theseus alive, she smiled with relief. "You did it!" she exclaimed. "I knew you would!"

But their victory was bittersweet. Theseus knew that King Minos would be furious when he found out that the Minotaur had been slain. It wouldn't be long before he sought revenge. So, Ariadne and Theseus came up with a plan to escape Crete together.

That night, under the cover of darkness, Theseus, Ariadne, and the other Athenians slipped away from the palace and boarded a ship, sailing away from Crete and back toward Athens.

For the first time in years, the people of Athens were free from the terror of the Minotaur, and it was all thanks to Theseus's courage, Ariadne's cleverness, and their teamwork.

What We Learn from Theseus

Theseus's story is more than just an exciting adventure—it's also filled with important lessons that we can all learn from. Let's take a look at some of the key takeaways from Theseus's battle with the Minotaur.

1. Overcoming Challenges with Courage

One of the most important lessons we learn from Theseus is the value of **courage**. The idea of entering the Labyrinth and facing the Minotaur was terrifying, but Theseus didn't let his fear stop him. He knew that it was his responsibility to protect his people, and he was willing to risk his life to do so.

In our own lives, we all face challenges that seem scary or overwhelming. But like Theseus, we can overcome those challenges if we face them with courage and determination. Even when things seem impossible, bravery can help us push forward and achieve our goals.

2. The Importance of Allies and Teamwork

While Theseus was a strong and skilled hero, he couldn't have succeeded without help. Ariadne's quick thinking and the thread she gave Theseus were just as important to his victory as his own strength and bravery. This teaches us the value of **teamwork** and **trust**. We don't always have to face challenges alone—sometimes, we need to rely on the help of others to succeed.

In life, it's important to recognize the value of working together with others. Whether it's a friend, family member, or teammate, having allies can make a big difference when we're facing difficult challenges.

3. Standing Up for What is Right

Theseus's decision to enter the Labyrinth wasn't just about defeating the Minotaur—it was about standing up for what was right. He couldn't bear to see the people of Athens suffer any longer, and he was willing to do whatever it took to stop the unfair tribute to Crete.

This teaches us the importance of standing up for justice and fairness, even when it's difficult. In our own lives, we may face situations where we see something wrong happening. Theseus's story reminds us that we should always strive to do what's right, even if it means taking risks.

4. Using Intelligence as Well as Strength

Theseus didn't defeat the Minotaur with brute force alone—he used his **intelligence** to navigate the Labyrinth and outsmart the beast. This is an important reminder that being smart and thinking things through is just as valuable as being strong or brave.

In life, it's important to use our brains to solve problems, just like Theseus did. Whether it's figuring out how to study for a test or finding a way to help a friend, thinking carefully and planning ahead can help us succeed.

Conclusion: A Hero's Journey

Theseus's journey into the Labyrinth is one of the greatest stories of courage, teamwork, and intelligence in Greek mythology. He faced a terrifying monster, overcame an impossible challenge, and freed his people from years of suffering. With the help of Ariadne and his own bravery, Theseus became a hero not just for Athens, but for all of Greece.

As we move forward in our journey through Greek mythology, take a moment to think about Theseus's story and how the lessons he learned apply to your own life. What challenges are you facing, and how can you use courage, intelligence, and teamwork to overcome them?

In the next chapter, we'll dive into the world of another famous Greek hero, and discover new lessons about bravery, strength, and friendship. But for now, let Theseus's story inspire you to face your own "Minotaurs" with confidence and courage.

Chapter Four

Hercules – The 12 Labors of the World's Strongest Hero

Hercules—just the name alone brings to mind images of incredible strength, towering monsters, and heroic battles. In this chapter, we're going to dive deep into the life of **Hercules**, the strongest hero in all of Greek mythology. From his amazing strength to the tragic events that led him to undertake his **12 Labors**, Hercules's story is one filled with triumph, heartbreak, and lessons about perseverance.

The Legend of Hercules

Hercules was not an ordinary man—he was the son of **Zeus**, the king of the gods, and a mortal woman named **Alcmene**. This made Hercules a **demigod**, which means he had the strength of a god but still faced the struggles of being human. Even as a baby,

Hercules showed signs of his incredible power. When **Hera**, Zeus's wife, learned of Hercules's birth, she became jealous. To make sure that he would never become a threat to the gods, Hera sent two **giant snakes** to kill baby Hercules in his crib. But Hercules, even as a newborn, grabbed the snakes and strangled them with his bare hands!

As Hercules grew older, his strength became legendary. He could lift enormous boulders, defeat wild beasts with his bare hands, and perform feats that no other mortal could. But his life wasn't always easy. Hera's jealousy of Hercules didn't fade as he grew up. She constantly plotted against him, hoping to ruin his life. And unfortunately, her plans eventually succeeded.

The Tragedy Behind the 12 Labors

One day, Hera cast a terrible spell on Hercules, driving him into a fit of uncontrollable rage. In his madness, Hercules did something he would regret for the rest of his life—he accidentally harmed his own family. When he regained his senses and realized what he had done, Hercules was devastated. Filled with grief and guilt, he sought advice from the

Oracle of Delphi to find out how he could atone for his actions.

The oracle told him that in order to cleanse himself of this terrible guilt, he would need to complete **12 impossible tasks**, known as the **12 Labors**. These tasks were designed to be so difficult that no ordinary man could complete them. But Hercules wasn't ordinary—he was determined to face each challenge, no matter how dangerous, and prove his worth.

Thus began Hercules's journey through the 12 Labors, each one more dangerous than the last. With every labor, Hercules faced terrifying creatures, impossible odds, and his own inner demons. But through it all, he showed incredible strength, courage, and perseverance.

Famous Labors: The Nemean Lion, the Hydra, and the Golden Apples

While all 12 of Hercules's Labors were impressive, there are three that stand out as the most famous and exciting: his battle with the **Nemean Lion**, his fight against the many-headed **Hydra**, and his quest to find the **Golden Apples of the Hesperides**. Let's take a closer look at each of these legendary challenges.

The Nemean Lion

Hercules's first labor was to defeat the **Nemean Lion**, a monstrous beast that terrorized the countryside of **Nemea**. The lion was no ordinary animal—its **fur was so thick and tough** that no weapon could pierce it. Arrows, swords, and spears all bounced off its hide, leaving the people of Nemea helpless against the lion's attacks.

When Hercules arrived in Nemea, he quickly realized that brute force alone wouldn't be enough to defeat the lion. After attempting to shoot arrows at the beast with no success, Hercules devised a clever plan. He chased the lion into its cave, trapping it inside with no escape route. Then, in a fierce battle, Hercules used his immense strength to wrestle the lion and **strangled it with his bare hands**.

After defeating the lion, Hercules used the lion's own **sharp claws** to cut through its tough hide and made a cloak out of its skin. From that day on, he wore the Nemean Lion's pelt as a symbol of his victory, and it became one of his most recognizable features.

The Hydra

The second labor of Hercules was even more dangerous than the first. He was tasked with slaying the **Hydra**, a fearsome creature with **nine heads**, one of which was immortal. But there was a catch—every time Hercules cut off one of the Hydra's heads, **two more would grow back** in its place. This meant that no matter how many times he attacked, the Hydra would just keep growing stronger.

Hercules traveled to the swamp where the Hydra lived, accompanied by his nephew **Iolaus**. As he approached the creature's lair, the Hydra rose out of the water, its many heads snapping and hissing in fury. Hercules knew that his usual strength wouldn't be enough to defeat this monster, so he had to use strategy.

With his trusty sword, Hercules began cutting off the Hydra's heads, but just as expected, two new heads sprouted in place of each one he removed. It seemed like an impossible task, but Hercules didn't give up. With Iolaus's help, they came up with a brilliant plan. After cutting off each head, Iolaus used a **torch** to **cauterize the wound**, preventing new heads from growing. Together, they worked swiftly, and soon, all of the Hydra's mortal heads were destroyed.

But the battle wasn't over yet. Hercules still had to deal with the **immortal head**, which could not be killed. Using his incredible strength, he crushed the immortal head under a massive boulder, trapping it forever.

Once the Hydra was defeated, Hercules dipped his arrows in the creature's **poisonous blood**, making them deadly weapons that would help him in future battles.

The Golden Apples of the Hesperides

One of the most famous and challenging labors was Hercules's quest to find the **Golden Apples of the Hesperides**. These apples were said to be **magical** and were kept in a beautiful garden, guarded by the **Hesperides**, nymphs who were daughters of the evening star, and a fearsome, hundred-headed dragon named **Ladon**.

The problem was that no one knew exactly where the garden was located—it was hidden far away, beyond the reach of most mortals. But Hercules was not easily discouraged. He set off on a long and dangerous journey, traveling to the farthest corners of the world in search of the apples.

Along the way, Hercules encountered many obstacles, including the **giant Atlas**, who held up the sky on his shoulders. Atlas knew where the garden was, but he didn't want to tell Hercules for free. Instead, he offered to get the apples for Hercules—if Hercules would hold up the sky in his place.

Hercules agreed, using his immense strength to support the weight of the heavens while Atlas went to retrieve the apples. But when Atlas returned, he decided that he didn't want to take the sky back—he planned to leave Hercules holding the sky forever!

But Hercules, always clever, tricked Atlas. He asked Atlas to take the sky back for just a moment so that he could adjust his grip. Atlas, not realizing the trick, agreed, and as soon as the sky was back on Atlas's shoulders, Hercules grabbed the golden apples and made his escape.

With the apples in hand, Hercules completed his labor and brought the magical fruit back as proof of his victory.

What We Learn from Hercules

Hercules's story is one of the most famous in all of mythology, not just because of his incredible strength, but because of the **lessons** we can learn from his journey. His 12 Labors teach us valuable lessons about perseverance, bravery, and the importance of learning from our mistakes.

1. Perseverance in the Face of Hardship

Perhaps the greatest lesson we learn from Hercules is the value of **perseverance**. Each of his labors was designed to be impossible, yet Hercules faced every challenge head-on, refusing to give up even when the odds seemed stacked against him. Whether he was wrestling the Nemean Lion or battling the Hydra, Hercules pushed forward with determination and strength.

In our own lives, we will face challenges that seem overwhelming or impossible to overcome. But just like Hercules, we can find the strength to persevere if we stay determined and never give up.

2. Even Heroes Make Mistakes

Hercules is often seen as the ultimate hero, but his story also teaches us that even heroes can make mistakes. His tragic error, caused by Hera's spell, led to his greatest hardship—the need to complete the 12 Labors. Hercules's story reminds us that no one is perfect, and even the strongest among us can stumble. But what's important is how we deal with those mistakes.

Hercules didn't let his error define him. Instead, he worked tirelessly to atone for his actions and prove himself worthy of the title of hero. This teaches us that while we all make mistakes, we have the power to learn from them and become better people.

3. Bravery and Strength Are Not Always Enough

While Hercules was known for his **incredible strength**, his labors show that **bravery** and **strategy** are just as important. He used his intelligence to defeat the Hydra and trick Atlas into giving him the golden apples. This reminds us that being strong is important, but sometimes, we also need to rely on our brains to solve problems.

In our lives, it's important to remember that while courage and hard work are essential, we should also think carefully about how to approach difficult situations.

Conclusion: A Hero's Journey of Strength and Wisdom

Hercules's journey through the 12 Labors is one of the greatest stories of heroism in Greek mythology. His immense strength, combined with his clever thinking, helped him overcome impossible odds and earn his place among the gods. But perhaps the most important part of Hercules's story is that he was not perfect—he made mistakes, but he never stopped working to make things right.

As we finish this chapter, take a moment to think about the challenges you face in your own life. How can you use the lessons from Hercules's journey to persevere, learn from your mistakes, and approach problems with both strength and wisdom?

Next, we'll meet more heroes and discover new lessons in the world of Greek mythology. But for now, let Hercules's story inspire you to face your own "Labors" with courage, intelligence, and determination.

Chapter Five

The Mythical Creatures of Ancient Greece

Greek mythology is not just about gods and heroes; it's also filled with incredible, fearsome, and mysterious **creatures**. These beings played important roles in the adventures of many heroes, acting as both obstacles to overcome and lessons to learn. Some of these creatures were terrifying beasts that tested the courage and strength of the greatest heroes, while others were tricky and sly, using deception to ensnare their prey.

In this chapter, we're going to meet some of the most famous and fearsome creatures in Greek mythology, including the **Minotaur**, the **Cyclops**, **Cerberus**, the **Sirens**, and the **Harpies**. These creatures might have been monstrous, but they all served to teach important lessons about bravery, wisdom, and the human spirit.

Meet the Minotaur, Cyclops, and Cerberus

The Minotaur – The Beast of the Labyrinth

We've already learned about the **Minotaur** in Theseus's story, but let's take a closer look at this terrifying creature and its significance in Greek mythology. The Minotaur had the body of a man and the head of a bull, a monstrous combination that made it one of the most feared creatures in all of Greece.

The Minotaur lived in the **Labyrinth**, a complex maze built by the brilliant inventor **Daedalus** on the island of **Crete**. The creature was kept there by **King Minos**, who fed the Minotaur human sacrifices—innocent youths and maidens sent from Athens as part of a cruel tribute. The Minotaur represented a blend of human intelligence and animalistic savagery, making it a symbol of the untamed and violent parts of nature.

Theseus's journey into the Labyrinth to slay the Minotaur wasn't just about killing a monster; it was about overcoming a fearsome enemy that combined both physical power and the confusing, disorienting maze of the Labyrinth itself. The story of the Minotaur teaches us about the importance of courage and strategy when faced with overwhelming odds.

The Cyclops – One-Eyed Giants

The **Cyclopes** (plural for **Cyclops**) were giant beings with only one eye in the center of their foreheads. These creatures were known for their incredible strength but also for their **simple-mindedness**. While there were several Cyclopes in Greek mythology, the most famous one is **Polyphemus**, who appeared in the story of **Odysseus**.

When Odysseus and his men were on their journey home from the Trojan War, they landed on the island where Polyphemus lived. Unfortunately, the giant captured them and trapped them in his cave, planning to eat them one by one. Polyphemus was strong, but he was not very clever, and this gave Odysseus a chance to escape. Odysseus and his men used their intelligence to trick the Cyclops, blinding his single eye and sneaking out of the cave by hiding underneath Polyphemus's sheep as they left to graze.

The Cyclops is often seen as a symbol of **raw strength without wisdom**. While Polyphemus was physically powerful, he was no match for Odysseus's cleverness. This teaches us that brains can be more valuable than brawn in tricky situations.

Cerberus – The Three-Headed Guard Dog

Guarding the gates of the **Underworld** was the fearsome **Cerberus**, a giant dog with **three heads**. Cerberus's job was to make sure that no one could leave the land of the dead. He was fiercely loyal to **Hades**, the god of the Underworld, and his role was to keep the living from entering the Underworld and the dead from escaping.

Cerberus was one of the most difficult obstacles that heroes faced when they ventured into the Underworld. **Hercules**, during his 12 Labors, had to capture Cerberus as one of his tasks. This was no easy feat, as Cerberus was not only powerful but also terrifying. However, Hercules managed to subdue the creature using his strength and courage, proving once again that he was capable of achieving even the most impossible tasks.

In many ways, Cerberus represents the **boundaries** between life and death. His three heads are often seen as a symbol of the past, present, and future, guarding the secrets of the Underworld and ensuring that the natural order of life and death is preserved.

The Sirens and the Harpies

The Sirens – Singers of Doom

The **Sirens** were beautiful, mysterious creatures known for their **enchanting voices**. They lived on rocky islands, and their song was so irresistible that sailors passing by couldn't help but steer their ships toward the sound, often leading them to their doom as their ships crashed onto the rocks. The Sirens' songs were a deadly temptation, luring sailors to their deaths.

One of the most famous stories involving the Sirens comes from **Odysseus's** journey home. Odysseus knew about the Sirens and their deadly songs, so he came up with a clever plan to protect himself and his crew. He ordered his men to plug their ears with beeswax so they wouldn't hear the Sirens' voices, but he wanted to hear their song himself. So, he had his men tie him to the mast of the ship, instructing them not to untie him no matter how much he begged. As they sailed past the Sirens, Odysseus heard their beautiful voices, but thanks to his plan, he and his crew survived.

The Sirens represent the danger of **temptation** and the importance of **self-control**. Their beauty and enchanting voices symbolize the allure of things that might seem appealing but can ultimately lead to harm. The lesson we learn from the Sirens is that wisdom and planning can help us resist dangerous temptations.

The Harpies – Winged Thieves

The **Harpies** were **winged creatures** with the bodies of birds and the heads of women. They were known for their ability to swoop down from the sky and snatch away anything they wanted—whether it was food, treasure, or even people. The Harpies were not as beautiful as the Sirens; in fact, they were often depicted as ugly and terrifying creatures.

In one famous myth, the Harpies tormented a king named **Phineus**. Every time Phineus tried to eat, the Harpies would swoop down and steal his food, leaving him starving. Phineus was eventually rescued by the **Argonauts**, a group of heroes led by **Jason**. They chased the Harpies away, freeing Phineus from their torment.

The Harpies represent the destructive power of **greed** and the importance of **fighting for what's right**. While they were not as seductive as the Sirens, the Harpies were just as dangerous in their own way, using their speed and trickery to steal what didn't belong to them.

What We Learn from Monsters

While the monsters of Greek mythology might seem terrifying, they all serve a greater purpose. Each of these creatures teaches us valuable lessons about **fear**, **courage**, and the human spirit. Let's take a look at some of the key lessons we can learn from these mythical beasts.

1. Facing Fear with Courage

Whether it's the Minotaur, the Cyclops, or Cerberus, many of the creatures in Greek mythology were designed to invoke fear. Heroes like Theseus, Odysseus, and Hercules didn't back down when faced with these terrifying monsters. Instead, they showed incredible courage in the face of fear, proving that bravery can overcome even the most daunting challenges.

In our own lives, we will face situations that seem scary or overwhelming. The monsters of Greek mythology remind us that fear is a natural part of life, but it's how we deal with that fear that defines us. Like the heroes, we can find the strength to face our fears head-on.

2. The Power of Intelligence and Strategy

While strength is important, many of the heroes in Greek mythology used their **intelligence** and **strategy** to defeat monsters. Odysseus outsmarted the Cyclops by using his cleverness, and he resisted the Sirens' deadly song through careful planning. These stories remind us that sometimes, being smart is just as important as being strong.

When faced with a difficult situation, we can use our brains to come up with solutions. Thinking things through, making a plan, and being clever can help us overcome even the trickiest obstacles.

3. Resisting Temptation and Making Wise Choices

The Sirens and the Harpies serve as symbols of **temptation**. Their alluring songs and sneaky behavior show us how easy it is to be tempted by things that seem appealing but can ultimately cause harm. Odysseus's story teaches us that wisdom and self-control are essential when dealing with temptation.

In life, we're often faced with choices that can seem exciting or tempting but may not be the best for us in the long run. The lessons from these creatures remind us to stay focused, think carefully about our decisions, and resist the pull of things that might lead us astray.

Conclusion: Lessons from Mythical Beasts

The monsters of Greek mythology are more than just fearsome creatures—they are symbols of the challenges and struggles that we all face in life. Whether it's overcoming fear, using intelligence, or resisting temptation, these creatures and their stories offer important lessons that are still relevant today.

As we continue our journey through the myths of ancient Greece, take a moment to think about the lessons these monsters can teach us. How can we face our own "monsters" with courage, wisdom, and determination?

Next up, we'll dive into the epic adventures of another legendary hero. But for now, let the stories of the Minotaur, the Cyclops, and the Sirens remind you that even the scariest challenges can be overcome with the right mindset.

Part 3

Epic Quests and Legendary Adventures

Chapter Six

Jason and the Argonauts – The Quest for the Golden Fleece

The story of **Jason and the Argonauts** is one of the greatest adventures in all of Greek mythology. It's a tale of bravery, teamwork, and a dangerous journey across the seas in search of the legendary **Golden Fleece**. This chapter will take us on a thrilling voyage with Jason and his band of heroic adventurers as they face incredible challenges, monstrous creatures, and nearly impossible odds.

Let's set sail with Jason and the Argonauts and explore the lessons they learned along the way about courage, leadership, and the power of working together.

The Journey of Jason and His Heroes

Our story begins in the ancient kingdom of **Iolcus**, where Jason was born. Jason's life wasn't always easy. As a baby, his uncle **Pelias** took the throne from Jason's father, **Aeson**, and became the king of Iolcus. Pelias was a cruel ruler, and he feared that one day Jason would return to claim the throne.

Years later, when Jason had grown into a strong and brave young man, he returned to Iolcus to demand his rightful place as king. Pelias, fearing Jason's claim, agreed to give up the throne—but only on one condition. He sent Jason on an impossible mission: to retrieve the **Golden Fleece**, a magical fleece that had the power to bring prosperity to its owner.

The Golden Fleece was said to be kept in a distant land called **Colchis**, guarded by a fierce dragon and nearly impossible to reach. Pelias was sure that Jason would never survive the journey. But Jason wasn't afraid. He accepted the challenge, determined to prove himself and bring the Golden Fleece back to Iolcus.

Assembling the Argonauts

Jason knew that he couldn't complete the journey alone. He needed the best and bravest heroes in all of Greece to help him. So, he assembled a group of legendary warriors, sailors, and adventurers, known as the **Argonauts**. These heroes included:

- **Hercules**, the strongest man in the world.
- **Orpheus**, a musician with the power to charm anything with his music.
- **Atalanta**, the fastest runner in Greece and a skilled huntress.
- **Castor and Pollux**, twin brothers known for their incredible fighting skills.
- **Meleager**, a fearless warrior.

Together, they set sail on the ship **Argo**, named after its builder, **Argus**. With Jason as their leader, the Argonauts embarked on a dangerous and thrilling journey across the seas, facing numerous challenges and obstacles along the way.

The Trials Along the Way

As with any great adventure, the journey to Colchis was filled with dangers, trials, and challenges that tested the courage and strength of Jason and his crew. Let's dive into some of the most famous trials they faced on their quest for the Golden Fleece.

The Harpies

One of the first challenges the Argonauts encountered was the terrifying **Harpies**, monstrous winged creatures that tormented a blind king named **Phineus**. The Harpies would swoop down and steal Phineus's food, leaving him to starve.

When Jason and the Argonauts arrived at Phineus's kingdom, they saw the terrible condition he was in and decided to help. The Harpies were fast and vicious, but the Argonauts were faster. With the help of the winged sons of the North Wind, **Zetes** and **Calais**, the Argonauts chased the Harpies away, freeing Phineus from their torment.

In gratitude, Phineus revealed to Jason a secret that would help him on his journey: the location of the

Clashing Rocks and how to pass through them safely.

The Clashing Rocks

The **Clashing Rocks**, also known as the **Symplegades**, were one of the most dangerous parts of the journey. These massive rocks stood at the entrance to a narrow strait, and every time a ship tried to pass through, the rocks would crash together, smashing anything in their way.

Phineus had warned Jason that the only way to pass through the Clashing Rocks was to send a **dove** through first. If the dove made it through, the ship could follow safely. If the dove was crushed, it meant the rocks were too dangerous to pass.

Following Phineus's advice, Jason sent a dove through the rocks, holding his breath as the rocks began to close. The dove flew swiftly, barely making it through with only a few feathers lost. Seeing this, Jason commanded the Argonauts to row with all their might, and with great speed and skill, the Argo sailed through the rocks just before they crashed together again.

The Clashing Rocks were a symbol of the dangers of the unknown, but with courage, strategy, and teamwork, Jason and his crew overcame the challenge and continued their journey.

Medea's Help

Finally, after many weeks of sailing and facing dangerous challenges, Jason and the Argonauts arrived in **Colchis**, the land of the Golden Fleece. But retrieving the fleece wouldn't be easy—it was guarded by a **fierce dragon** that never slept, and the king of Colchis, **Aeëtes**, had no intention of giving it up without a fight.

However, Jason found an unexpected ally in Aeëtes's daughter, **Medea**. Medea was a powerful sorceress, skilled in magic and potions. She fell in love with Jason and offered to help him retrieve the Golden Fleece, even though it meant betraying her own father.

Medea gave Jason a magical **potion** that would make him strong enough to face the challenges ahead. She also told him how to defeat the dragon that guarded the fleece. With her help, Jason approached the dragon, using the potion to put the creature to sleep. Then, with great care, he took the **Golden Fleece** from the tree where it hung and claimed it as his own.

But their troubles were far from over. King Aeëtes was furious when he discovered that Jason had taken the fleece and that Medea had helped him. He sent his soldiers to capture Jason and the Argonauts, but Medea, using her magic, helped the heroes escape.

Jason, Medea, and the Argonauts sailed away from Colchis, their quest for the Golden Fleece complete. But their journey wasn't over yet. They still had to return to Iolcus, where Jason would claim his throne.

What We Learn from Jason

Jason's quest for the Golden Fleece is more than just a thrilling adventure—it's also a story filled with valuable lessons about leadership, teamwork, and the importance of bravery in the face of danger.

Let's explore some of the important takeaways from Jason's journey.

1. The Value of Teamwork

Jason knew from the very beginning that he couldn't complete the quest alone. He needed the help of brave and skilled companions, each of whom brought something unique to the table. Whether it was the strength of Hercules, the musical talents of Orpheus, or the hunting skills of Atalanta, every member of the Argonauts played a role in their success.

The story of Jason and the Argonauts reminds us that no one can achieve great things alone. **Teamwork** is essential, and when we work together, we can accomplish amazing feats.

2. The Importance of Leadership

As the leader of the Argonauts, Jason had to make difficult decisions throughout the journey. He was responsible for the safety of his crew, and he had to be brave, smart, and fair in order to earn their trust and respect. His leadership was crucial in guiding the Argonauts through the many challenges they faced.

This teaches us that being a good leader means not just having courage, but also knowing when to listen to others, make tough choices, and inspire those around you to work together toward a common goal.

3. Facing Fears and Overcoming Challenges

From the Clashing Rocks to the dragon guarding the Golden Fleece, Jason and the Argonauts faced many terrifying challenges. But instead of running away, they used their wits, their courage, and their teamwork to face each challenge head-on.

In life, we will all face obstacles that seem impossible to overcome. The story of Jason reminds us that with **bravery**, **strategy**, and the support of others, we can face our fears and achieve our goals.

Conclusion: A Legendary Adventure

Jason's quest for the Golden Fleece is one of the most famous stories in all of Greek mythology, and for good reason. It's a tale of incredible adventure, fierce battles, and the power of teamwork. Through Jason's leadership and the bravery of the Argonauts, we learn that even the most impossible challenges can be overcome when we work together and face our fears.

As we continue our journey through Greek mythology, let Jason's story inspire you to lead with courage, value your teammates, and face your challenges with confidence. The next chapter will take us into more heroic adventures, but for now, let's celebrate the victory of Jason and the Argonauts in retrieving the Golden Fleece.

Chapter Seven

Odysseus – The Epic Journey of the Odyssey

In Greek mythology, few stories are as thrilling and legendary as the **Odyssey**, the epic journey of **Odysseus**. After fighting for ten long years in the Trojan War, Odysseus's return home wasn't simple or straightforward. His journey stretched another **ten years**, filled with dangerous creatures, treacherous gods, and mythical challenges that tested both his strength and cleverness.

Odysseus wasn't just a warrior—he was known for his **intelligence**, **resourcefulness**, and his ability to outsmart even the trickiest opponents. In this chapter, we'll follow Odysseus through his incredible adventures and see how he used his wit and cunning to survive the many dangers that stood in his way.

Odysseus's Return from the Trojan War

The story of Odysseus begins at the end of the **Trojan War**, a long and brutal conflict between the Greeks and the city of **Troy**. Thanks to Odysseus's clever idea to build the famous **Trojan Horse**, the Greeks were able to sneak into the city of Troy and win the war. But as soon as the war ended, Odysseus's troubles began.

Odysseus's homeland was the island of **Ithaca**, where his wife, **Penelope**, and his young son, **Telemachus**, were waiting for him to return. Odysseus longed to go home and be reunited with his family, but the journey was filled with danger. The gods were angry with him, especially **Poseidon**, the god of the sea, who decided to make Odysseus's voyage home as difficult as possible.

The Cyclops

One of the first major challenges that Odysseus and his men faced on their journey was the **Cyclops**, a one-eyed giant named **Polyphemus**. After landing on an unknown island, Odysseus and his men came across a cave filled with food and supplies. Hungry and tired, they helped themselves to the Cyclops's provisions, not knowing that they were in great danger.

When Polyphemus returned to his cave and discovered the intruders, he was furious. The giant trapped Odysseus and his men inside the cave by rolling a huge boulder in front of the entrance, and one by one, Polyphemus began to eat Odysseus's men.

Odysseus knew that he couldn't fight the Cyclops with brute force, so he came up with a plan. First, he offered Polyphemus **wine**, and when the Cyclops became drunk and drowsy, Odysseus told him that his name was "**Nobody**." Then, while the Cyclops slept, Odysseus and his remaining men sharpened a large wooden stake and **blinded** Polyphemus by driving the stake into his single eye.

When Polyphemus cried out in pain, the other Cyclopes on the island came to see what was wrong. But when they asked who had attacked him, Polyphemus could only shout, "Nobody is hurting me!" Thinking he was unharmed, the other Cyclopes left, and Odysseus's clever trick worked.

But they still had to escape from the cave. Polyphemus, now blind, sat at the entrance, feeling for anyone trying to leave. Odysseus came up with another clever plan—he tied his men under the bellies of **sheep**, and when Polyphemus let the sheep out to graze, he couldn't feel the men hiding underneath them. In this way, Odysseus and his crew escape the Cyclops's cave and continue their journey.

The Sirens

As Odysseus's journey continued, he and his men faced another deadly challenge—the **Sirens**. The Sirens were beautiful, mysterious creatures with voices so enchanting that sailors couldn't resist their songs. But their sweet music was a deadly trap—anyone who tried to follow the Sirens' voices would end up crashing their ship on the rocky shores where the Sirens lived.

Odysseus knew that they would be sailing past the Sirens' island, so he came up with a plan to save his men. He ordered his crew to plug their ears with **beeswax** so they wouldn't hear the Sirens' voices. But Odysseus, always curious, wanted to hear the Sirens' song for himself. So he had his men **tie him to the mast** of the ship, instructing them not to untie him, no matter how much he begged.

As they sailed past the island, the Sirens began to sing their haunting, beautiful song. Odysseus was mesmerized and pleaded with his men to let him go, but they followed his orders and kept him tied up until they were safely past the island. Thanks to

Odysseus's clever plan, the crew survived the Sirens' deadly temptation.

Scylla and Charybdis

As if the journey wasn't already dangerous enough, Odysseus and his men soon found themselves between two of the most feared creatures in the sea—**Scylla** and **Charybdis**. Scylla was a monster with six long necks, each ending in a head with sharp teeth, while Charybdis was a giant whirlpool that swallowed entire ships whole.

Odysseus had to make a terrible choice: sail too close to Scylla, and some of his men would be snatched and eaten by the monster, or sail too close to Charybdis and risk losing the entire ship to the whirlpool. In the end, Odysseus chose to sail near Scylla, sacrificing a few men to save the rest of the crew.

It was a heartbreaking decision, but Odysseus knew that sometimes, even heroes have to make difficult choices. With a heavy heart, he guided his ship past

Scylla and Charybdis, continuing the journey toward Ithaca.

The Cleverness of Odysseus

Odysseus wasn't just known for his strength—what made him a legendary hero was his **cleverness**. Time and time again, he used his **intelligence** and **resourcefulness** to overcome the challenges he faced. Whether it was outwitting the Cyclops, resisting the temptation of the Sirens, or making difficult decisions in the face of danger, Odysseus proved that being smart is just as important as being strong.

One of the greatest examples of Odysseus's cleverness came at the end of his long journey, when he finally returned home to Ithaca. After twenty years away, he found that his palace had been taken over by a group of suitors who were trying to marry his wife, **Penelope**, thinking that Odysseus was dead.

Instead of barging in and fighting the suitors head-on, Odysseus came up with a clever plan. He disguised himself as a beggar and secretly entered the palace. Only a few people, including his loyal servant **Eurycleia** and his son, Telemachus, recognized him.

Odysseus then revealed himself to Penelope by completing a challenge that only he could accomplish—stringing his old bow and shooting an arrow through twelve axeheads, a feat that required incredible strength and skill. Once his identity was revealed, Odysseus and Telemachus fought off the suitors and reclaimed the palace.

Through it all, Odysseus's cleverness and ability to think on his feet were what helped him survive and succeed. His journey home was filled with impossible challenges, but he never gave up, using his wits to outsmart the obstacles in his way.

What We Learn from Odysseus

The story of Odysseus is filled with exciting adventures and dangerous challenges, but it also teaches us important lessons about intelligence, bravery, and perseverance. Let's take a closer look at what we can learn from the clever hero of the Odyssey.

1. Intelligence and Resourcefulness Are Just as Important as Strength

One of the most important lessons we learn from Odysseus is that being smart is just as valuable as being strong. While many Greek heroes were known for their physical strength, Odysseus's true power came from his intelligence and ability to outthink his enemies.

Whether it was escaping from the Cyclops's cave or resisting the Sirens' song, Odysseus used his brain to come up with clever solutions to the problems he faced. This teaches us that in life, we should always try to think things through and find creative solutions to our challenges. Sometimes, being clever is the best way to succeed.

2. Perseverance in the Face of Adversity

Odysseus's journey home wasn't easy—it took him ten long years to return to Ithaca after the Trojan War, and along the way, he faced many trials that seemed impossible to overcome. But no matter how difficult things became, Odysseus never gave up. He kept moving forward, determined to make it home to his family.

This teaches us the importance of **perseverance**. In life, we will face challenges that seem overwhelming, but like Odysseus, we should keep pushing forward, even when the road ahead looks tough. Perseverance is the key to reaching our goals, no matter how far away they seem.

3. Facing Temptation with Wisdom

One of the most dangerous challenges Odysseus faced was the temptation of the Sirens. Their song was beautiful and enchanting, but following it would have led to disaster. Odysseus knew that he couldn't resist their song alone, so he came up with a plan to protect himself and his men.

This teaches us about the importance of **wisdom** and **self-control**. In life, we will face temptations that seem appealing, but we need to be wise enough to recognize when something might lead us astray. By thinking ahead and making smart decisions, we can avoid dangerous situations and stay on the right path.

Conclusion: A Journey of Cleverness and Courage

The story of Odysseus's journey home is one of the most famous and exciting adventures in all of Greek mythology. But more than just an epic tale, the Odyssey teaches us valuable lessons about intelligence, perseverance, and the power of clever thinking. Odysseus may not have been the strongest hero, but he proved time and time again that **cleverness** and **resourcefulness** can overcome even the greatest challenges.

As we continue our journey through the myths of ancient Greece, let Odysseus's story inspire you to think creatively, face your challenges with courage, and never give up, no matter how long the journey may be.

Part 4

The Underworld and the gods of Death

Chapter Eight

Hades, Persephone, and the Underworld

Greek mythology isn't just about the sky, the seas, and the earth—it also takes us deep into the mysterious world of the **Underworld**, the kingdom of the dead. But don't worry, even though the Underworld may sound spooky, it's also a fascinating place filled with powerful gods, important stories, and lessons about life and nature. In this chapter, we'll explore the realm of **Hades**, the god who rules the Underworld, and discover how his queen, **Persephone**, plays a key role in the changing seasons. We'll also meet **Cerberus**, the three-headed guard dog, and learn about the famous **River Styx**.

Let's dive into the depths of the Underworld and discover its secrets!

The Kingdom of the Dead

The Underworld is the place where the souls of the dead go after they leave the world of the living. While other gods like **Zeus** ruled the sky and **Poseidon** controlled the sea, it was **Hades**, the brother of Zeus and Poseidon, who ruled the Underworld. Hades wasn't an evil god—he was fair and just, making sure that the souls of the dead were taken care of. But because he ruled the realm of the dead, people often feared him.

Hades's kingdom was deep beneath the earth, hidden from the eyes of mortals. It was a vast, shadowy place filled with rivers, caverns, and secret passages. To enter the Underworld, souls had to cross the **River Styx**, a dark and powerful river that separated the world of the living from the world of the dead. But more on that later!

Persephone: Queen of the Underworld

While Hades ruled the Underworld, he wasn't alone. His wife, **Persephone**, was the **Queen of the Underworld**. But Persephone wasn't always the queen—her story is one of the most famous in Greek mythology, and it has everything to do with the changing seasons.

Persephone was the daughter of **Demeter**, the goddess of agriculture and harvest. She lived in the world above, where flowers bloomed and crops grew, and she spent her days happily wandering through meadows and fields. But everything changed when Hades saw Persephone and decided he wanted her to be his queen.

One day, while Persephone was picking flowers, Hades appeared from a crack in the earth, riding his chariot pulled by black horses. In a flash, he swept Persephone away to the Underworld, where he made her his queen. The sudden disappearance of Persephone left the world above in sadness and darkness, as her mother, Demeter, searched desperately for her lost daughter.

The Story of Persephone and the Changing Seasons

The story of **Persephone's abduction** by Hades doesn't just explain how she became the Queen of the Underworld—it also tells the story of why we have **seasons**. Let's explore this story in a kid-friendly way!

After Hades took Persephone to the Underworld, her mother, Demeter, was heartbroken. Demeter loved her daughter more than anything, and she was so sad that she couldn't take care of the plants and crops on Earth. Without Demeter's care, the plants withered, the fields turned dry, and no crops could grow. The world became cold and barren.

Zeus, the king of the gods, saw what was happening and realized that something had to be done. If Demeter continued to mourn, nothing would grow, and people would starve. So, he sent a message to Hades, telling him to return Persephone to her mother.

But there was one problem: while Persephone was in the Underworld, she had eaten **six pomegranate seeds**, and according to the ancient rules, anyone who ate the food of the dead had to stay in the Underworld forever. Hades agreed to let Persephone go back to the world above, but only for part of the year. For six months of the year, Persephone would live with her mother, and for the other six months, she would return to the Underworld to be with Hades.

This is how the seasons were created! When Persephone returns to her mother, **spring** arrives, and the world becomes warm and full of life. Flowers bloom, trees grow, and crops flourish because Demeter is happy. This lasts through the **summer**. But when Persephone must return to the Underworld, **fall** and **winter** come, and the world becomes cold and barren again, as Demeter mourns her daughter's absence.

So, the myth of Persephone explains why the seasons change, as her journey between the world above and the Underworld marks the cycle of growth, harvest, and rest.

The River Styx and Cerberus, the Three-Headed Guard Dog

Now that we've learned about Hades and Persephone, let's take a closer look at some of the most important features of the Underworld: the **River Styx** and the fearsome guard dog, **Cerberus**.

The River Styx

In Greek mythology, the River Styx was the boundary between the world of the living and the Underworld. When someone died, their soul had to cross this dark river to reach the land of the dead. But crossing the River Styx wasn't easy! Souls had to be ferried across by **Charon**, the ferryman of the dead. He would only take souls across if they had a proper **coin** placed on their mouth or in their hand when they were buried. Without a coin, the souls were doomed to wander the shores of the river for eternity.

The River Styx wasn't just a physical boundary—it also had magical powers. The gods took oaths by the river, and anyone who broke an oath sworn by the Styx would lose their immortality for a time. The river symbolized the unbreakable bond between life and death, and it was one of the most important parts of Hades's kingdom.

Cerberus: The Three-Headed Guard Dog

Standing at the gates of the Underworld, ensuring that no living soul could enter and no dead soul could escape, was the fearsome **Cerberus**. Cerberus was a gigantic dog with **three heads**, each one more ferocious than the last. His job was to guard the entrance to the Underworld, and he was incredibly loyal to Hades.

Despite his terrifying appearance, Cerberus wasn't evil—he was simply doing his job, protecting the Underworld from intruders. Only the bravest and cleverest of heroes could pass Cerberus, and few ever dared to try.

One of the few who succeeded was **Hercules**. During his **12 Labors**, Hercules was tasked with capturing Cerberus and bringing him to the world above. Using his incredible strength, Hercules managed to subdue Cerberus, though he didn't harm the creature. He simply borrowed him for a short time before returning him to his rightful place at the gates of the Underworld.

Cerberus's three heads are often seen as a symbol of the **past, present, and future**, guarding the secrets of the Underworld and keeping the natural order of life and death in balance.

What We Learn from the Underworld

The stories of Hades, Persephone, the River Styx, and Cerberus might seem dark at first, but they teach us important lessons about **life**, **death**, and the natural world. Let's take a look at some of the key lessons we can learn from the Underworld.

1. Life and Death as Part of a Natural Cycle

The story of Persephone and the changing seasons reminds us that **life** and **death** are part of a natural cycle. Just as winter gives way to spring, and night gives way to day, everything in the world has a time of growth and a time of rest. In the myth, Persephone's journey between the Underworld and the world above symbolizes this cycle, showing us that life is constantly moving and changing.

This teaches us to appreciate the different stages of life and to recognize that everything has its season. Even when things seem difficult or sad, like in the cold of winter, we can look forward to the new growth and warmth of spring.

2. The Importance of Respect and Balance

Hades's role as the ruler of the Underworld teaches us the importance of **balance** and **respect** for the forces of nature. While Hades was feared, he wasn't a villain—he simply maintained the balance between life and death, making sure that the natural order was preserved. The River Styx and Cerberus both serve to keep the boundaries between the worlds intact, showing us the importance of respecting the rules of life and death.

This reminds us that everything in life has its place, and it's important to respect the natural world and the cycles that keep everything in balance. Whether it's the changing of the seasons, the passing of time, or the forces of life and death, balance and respect are key to understanding the world around us.

Conclusion: The Underworld's Lessons of Life and Nature

The Underworld may seem like a mysterious and shadowy place, but it's also full of important lessons about life, death, and the natural world. From the story of Persephone and the changing seasons to the powerful presence of Cerberus and the River Styx, these myths show us that even in the darkest places, there are valuable lessons to be learned.

As we continue our journey through Greek mythology, let the story of the Underworld remind you to appreciate the cycles of nature, respect the forces of life, and always seek balance in everything you do.

Chapter Nine

Orpheus and Eurydice – A Love Story from the Underworld

In the world of Greek mythology, there are many stories about brave heroes, fearsome monsters, and powerful gods. But there's one story that stands out for its beauty, emotion, and tragedy—the story of **Orpheus and Eurydice**. This is a love story unlike any other, where the power of **music** and the strength of **love** bring a man to the depths of the **Underworld** in a desperate attempt to rescue the woman he loves.

Orpheus wasn't a warrior or a king. His gift wasn't his strength or his courage, but his incredible talent for music. With his magical **lyre**, Orpheus could charm anything and anyone—trees, animals, rivers, and even the gods themselves. His love for **Eurydice**, a beautiful nymph, was deep and pure. But their happiness was short-lived, and when tragedy struck, Orpheus's love would lead him on a journey to the Underworld, where the ultimate test of **trust** awaited him.

The Power of Music and Love

Orpheus was known across the land as the greatest musician to ever live. His music wasn't just beautiful—it was **magical**. When Orpheus played his lyre, the world seemed to stop and listen. Birds would pause in mid-flight, rivers would slow their rushing currents, and even the trees would lean closer to hear his enchanting melodies. Orpheus's music could move both mortals and gods, and his heart belonged to one person—**Eurydice**.

Orpheus and Eurydice were deeply in love, and their life together was filled with joy. But one day, tragedy struck. While walking in a meadow, Eurydice was bitten by a poisonous snake. The venom quickly spread through her body, and before anyone could save her, Eurydice died. Her soul descended to the Underworld, the land of the dead, leaving Orpheus heartbroken and devastated.

Orpheus couldn't bear the thought of living without Eurydice. Overcome with grief, he made a decision that few mortals had ever dared to make—he would journey to the Underworld to bring her back.

Orpheus knew that this would be no easy task, but his love for Eurydice was stronger than his fear of death.

Taking his lyre, Orpheus traveled to the entrance of the Underworld, where the souls of the dead passed after leaving the world of the living. He knew that the path ahead was dangerous and filled with challenges, but he believed that the power of his music would be his greatest ally.

As Orpheus entered the Underworld, he played his lyre, filling the dark and shadowy realm with beautiful, haunting melodies. His music reached the ears of **Charon**, the ferryman who carried souls across the **River Styx**. Normally, Charon only allowed the dead to board his boat, but when he heard Orpheus's music, he was so moved that he agreed to take Orpheus across the river.

Orpheus continued to play as he journeyed deeper into the Underworld. His music was so powerful that even the fearsome **Cerberus**, the three-headed guard dog of Hades, sat calmly and listened, allowing Orpheus to pass without harm. With every note, Orpheus charmed the creatures and spirits of the

Underworld, using his music to guide him closer to his beloved Eurydice.

Finally, Orpheus reached the throne of **Hades** and **Persephone**, the rulers of the Underworld. He stood before them, his heart full of sorrow, and played a song so full of love and longing that even the cold-hearted Hades was moved to pity. As the music filled the Underworld, the spirits wept, and for the first time, Hades felt the pain of loss.

When Orpheus finished his song, he spoke to Hades and Persephone. "I have come to bring Eurydice back to the world of the living," he said. "My love for her is stronger than death itself. Please, allow her to return with me."

Hades, who was not easily swayed, was deeply moved by Orpheus's devotion and the beauty of his music. He agreed to let Eurydice return with Orpheus, but he placed one condition on their journey back to the world of the living: **Orpheus must not look back** at Eurydice until they had both reached the surface. If he looked back before they were fully out of the Underworld, Eurydice would be lost to him forever.

The Lesson of Trust

With his heart full of hope, Orpheus set off on the journey back to the world above. Behind him, he could hear the soft footsteps of Eurydice as she followed him. He longed to turn around and see her face, but he remembered Hades's warning. As much as he wanted to make sure Eurydice was truly behind him, he knew that he had to trust in her presence and in the promise that she would be by his side once they returned to the surface.

The path out of the Underworld was long and winding. As Orpheus walked, doubts began to creep into his mind. What if Hades had tricked him? What if Eurydice wasn't really following him? The further they walked, the more Orpheus's heart was filled with uncertainty.

Finally, just as they were nearing the exit to the Underworld, Orpheus could no longer resist the urge to look back. He wanted to see Eurydice, to know for sure that she was with him. In that moment of doubt, Orpheus turned his head.

And there, standing behind him, was Eurydice—her face filled with love and sadness. But before Orpheus could say a word, Eurydice began to fade away, pulled back into the depths of the Underworld. Her final words to Orpheus echoed in the dark: "Farewell, my love."

Orpheus had broken the one rule Hades had set. By looking back, he lost Eurydice forever. She disappeared back into the shadows, and this time, there was no second chance. Heartbroken, Orpheus was forced to return to the world of the living alone.

What We Learn from Orpheus

The story of Orpheus and Eurydice is one of the most emotional and tragic tales in Greek mythology. It's a story about the power of **love**, but it's also a story about the importance of **trust**. Orpheus's journey to the Underworld shows us how far someone will go for love, but his failure to trust in the process ultimately led to his downfall. Let's explore some of the lessons we can learn from this heartbreaking tale.

1. Trust is Essential in Relationships

At its core, the story of Orpheus and Eurydice is about **trust**. Hades gave Orpheus a simple task: to walk out of the Underworld without looking back at Eurydice. But in the end, Orpheus couldn't trust that Eurydice was truly behind him. His doubt and insecurity caused him to break the one rule that would have allowed him to be reunited with her.

In relationships, whether they are between friends, family, or loved ones, **trust** is one of the most important elements. Without trust, doubt can creep in, and that doubt can lead to mistakes and misunderstandings. Orpheus's story reminds us that trust is essential for building and maintaining strong relationships.

2. The Power of Love and Music

Orpheus's music was so powerful that it could charm anyone—even the gods of the Underworld. His love for Eurydice was what gave him the strength to make the dangerous journey into the land of the dead, and it was his music that softened the heart of Hades.

This teaches us about the power of **love** and the ability of music, art, and creativity to touch people's hearts. Orpheus's music wasn't just a talent—it was an expression of his love, and it had the ability to bring beauty into even the darkest places. In our own lives, we can use our talents and creativity to bring joy and light to others.

3. The Pain of Loss and Letting Go

Orpheus's story is also about **loss**. Even though he came so close to saving Eurydice, he ultimately had to face the painful truth that she was gone forever. This part of the story teaches us that sometimes, no matter how hard we try, we cannot change certain things. Learning to let go, while difficult, is an important part of life.

Orpheus's journey through grief and loss reminds us that love can be a source of both joy and pain. But even in the face of loss, we can find strength in the memories and beauty that love brings into our lives.

Conclusion: A Story of Love and Trust

The story of **Orpheus and Eurydice** is one of the most touching and tragic tales in Greek mythology. It's a reminder that love can lead us to do incredible things, but it also teaches us the importance of **trust**. Orpheus's failure to trust in the process led to his heartbreaking loss, showing us that doubt can have serious consequences.

As we continue our journey through Greek mythology, let Orpheus's story remind you to trust in the people you love, appreciate the power of music and creativity, and remember that even in the face of loss, love is a force that brings beauty into the world.

Part 5

Learning from Myths – Lessons for Life

Chapter Ten

What Greek Myths Teach Us About Friendship, Bravery, and Curiosity

Greek myths have taken us on a journey filled with daring heroes, incredible creatures, and powerful gods. But these stories aren't just about ancient adventures—they also teach us important lessons about life that we can use every day. Whether it's **friendship**, **bravery**, or the spirit of **curiosity**, Greek myths offer valuable insights into how we can face challenges, work together, and explore the world around us.

In this final chapter, we'll reflect on the lessons these timeless myths teach us, and we'll see how we can apply them to our own lives. So let's dive in and discover what Greek myths have to say about friendship, bravery, and curiosity.

The Value of Friendship

Throughout Greek mythology, one thing is clear—no hero succeeds alone. Even the strongest and bravest heroes needed the help of their **friends** and companions to overcome challenges. Friendship is one of the most important themes in these myths, showing us that teamwork and trust in others are essential for achieving great things.

Theseus and the Power of Friendship

Let's start with the story of **Theseus**, who relied on the help of his friends and allies to defeat the **Minotaur** and navigate the **Labyrinth**. Theseus was brave, but without the help of **Ariadne**, who gave him the thread to find his way out, he might never have survived. This shows us that even the bravest heroes need support from others.

Another great example of friendship in action is the story of **Jason and the Argonauts**. Jason knew that he couldn't complete the quest for the **Golden Fleece** on his own, so he gathered a team of heroic friends—including **Hercules**, **Orpheus**, and

Atalanta—to sail with him on the **Argo**. Together, they faced dangerous creatures and treacherous challenges, but they succeeded because they worked as a team.

Hercules and the Support of Friends

Even the mighty **Hercules** needed the support of friends to complete his famous **12 Labors**. One of his closest companions was **Iolaus**, his nephew, who helped him defeat the **Hydra**. When Hercules cut off one of the Hydra's heads and two more grew back, Iolaus used a torch to burn the stumps, preventing new heads from forming. Without Iolaus's help, Hercules might not have completed this dangerous task.

The lesson we learn from Theseus, Jason, and Hercules is that **friendship** is one of the most powerful tools we have. Whether we're facing a difficult problem, a scary situation, or a big adventure, having friends by our side can make all the difference. Friends offer support, encouragement, and strength when we need it most, just like the companions in Greek myths.

Being Brave Even When You're Scared

Many of the heroes in Greek myths faced terrifying dangers—whether it was the **Cyclops**, the **Minotaur**, or the **Hydra**, these creatures were enough to make anyone afraid. But the heroes didn't let their fear stop them from moving forward. In fact, being brave doesn't mean you're never scared—it means pushing through your fear and doing what needs to be done, even when it's hard.

Odysseus's Courage

Odysseus, the clever hero of the **Odyssey**, faced many frightening challenges on his journey home from the Trojan War. Whether it was outsmarting the giant Cyclops or navigating past the deadly **Sirens**, Odysseus had plenty of reasons to be scared. But what made him a great hero wasn't that he was fearless—it was that he faced these dangers with **courage** and determination.

When Odysseus tied himself to the mast of his ship to resist the Sirens' song, he was protecting both himself and his crew. He knew the Sirens' song was tempting, but instead of giving in to his fear or curiosity, he made a plan to outsmart them. This teaches us that sometimes, being brave means preparing for challenges and finding ways to overcome them.

Perseus and Facing the Unknown

Another great example of bravery is the story of **Perseus**, who set out on a dangerous quest to slay **Medusa**, the Gorgon with snakes for hair who could turn people to stone with a single glance. Perseus must have been terrified as he entered Medusa's lair, but he didn't let that fear stop him. With the help of the gods and his clever use of a reflective shield, Perseus managed to defeat Medusa and return victorious.

The important lesson here is that **everyone feels afraid sometimes**, even the greatest heroes. But instead of running away, they find ways to face their fears and move forward. In our own lives, we might face situations that make us nervous or scared, but like the heroes of Greek mythology, we can find the courage to keep going.

Curiosity and Exploration

The heroes of Greek myths were **explorers**, always searching for new adventures and knowledge. Their curiosity about the world led them to discover new lands, solve problems, and learn important lessons. Greek mythology teaches us that being curious and asking questions is a good thing—it helps us learn more about the world and ourselves.

Jason's Quest for the Golden Fleece

Jason and the Argonauts didn't have to go on their dangerous voyage to find the **Golden Fleece**, but their curiosity and determination led them on one of the most exciting adventures in mythology. Along the way, they encountered mythical creatures, made new allies, and learned valuable lessons about leadership, teamwork, and perseverance.

Jason's journey shows us that **exploration** and **curiosity** can open doors to incredible adventures. Whether it's exploring new places, trying new things, or learning something new, being curious about the world can lead to amazing discoveries.

The Importance of Asking Questions

Greek myths also teach us the importance of **asking questions. Prometheus**, for example, was a titan who was curious about the world of mortals. His curiosity led him to give **fire** to humans, an act that changed the course of history. Though he faced punishment for his actions, Prometheus's desire to help humanity shows that curiosity, even when it leads to challenges, can be a force for good.

In our own lives, being curious means asking questions about the world around us. Why do things work the way they do? How can we make the world a better place? The more questions we ask, the more we learn, and the more we grow as individuals. Like the heroes of Greek mythology, we should never stop exploring and seeking knowledge.

Interactive Element: Reflecting on Myths

Now that we've explored the lessons from Greek mythology, let's take a moment to **reflect** on what we've learned. Think about the heroes, the creatures, and the challenges they faced. What do their stories mean to you? How can you apply their lessons in your own life? Here are some questions to help you reflect:

- **Friendship:**
    - In what ways have your friends helped you when you needed support?
    - How can you be a good friend to others, just like Theseus and Jason's companions?
- **Bravery:**
    - Have you ever faced a situation that made you feel afraid? How did you find the courage to keep going?
    - What can you learn from the bravery of Odysseus, Perseus, or Hercules?
- **Curiosity:**
    - What are you curious about? Is there something you want to learn or explore, just like Jason's quest for the Golden Fleece?
    - How can you use your curiosity to discover new things or solve problems?

Remember, the heroes of Greek mythology weren't perfect—they made mistakes, they faced fears, and they sometimes relied on others for help. But they kept moving forward, learning, and growing. You can do the same in your own life, applying the lessons of friendship, bravery, and curiosity to face whatever challenges come your way.

Conclusion: Applying the Lessons of Greek Myths

Greek myths are more than just exciting stories about gods, heroes, and monsters—they're stories that teach us about **life** and how to be our best selves. From the importance of **friendship** to the value of **bravery** and the power of **curiosity**, these myths offer lessons that are still relevant today.

As you continue your journey through life, remember the stories of **Theseus**, **Odysseus**, **Jason**, and all the other heroes who faced challenges, made friends, and explored the unknown. Their adventures can inspire you to be brave, to trust in your friends, and to stay curious about the world around you.

And always remember, just like the heroes of Greek mythology, you too have the power to overcome challenges, discover new things, and make a positive impact on the world.

Glossary of Mythological Terms

This **Glossary of Mythological Terms** is designed to help you understand the key characters, places, and concepts mentioned throughout the book. Here, you'll find simple definitions that make Greek mythology easier to understand and more accessible.

Aegeus: The father of Theseus, king of Athens. He is part of the story of Theseus's adventure to defeat the Minotaur.

Aeson: Jason's father, the rightful king of Iolcus. He was overthrown by his brother, Pelias, which set Jason on his quest for the Golden Fleece.

Ariadne: The daughter of King Minos of Crete who helped Theseus defeat the Minotaur by giving him a ball of thread to navigate the Labyrinth.

Argonauts: A group of heroes who accompanied Jason on his quest to find the Golden Fleece. The Argonauts included famous heroes like Hercules, Orpheus, and Atalanta.

Cerberus: The three-headed dog that guards the entrance to the Underworld, ensuring that no one enters or leaves without permission.

Charon: The ferryman who transports the souls of the dead across the River Styx to the Underworld. He requires a coin as payment for the journey.

Cyclops: A one-eyed giant. The most famous Cyclops is Polyphemus, whom Odysseus encounters on his journey home from the Trojan War.

Demeter: The goddess of agriculture and harvest. She is the mother of Persephone, and her grief over Persephone's time in the Underworld causes the changing of the seasons.

Eurydice: The wife of Orpheus, who dies from a snake bite. Orpheus attempts to rescue her from the Underworld using the power of his music.

Golden Fleece: A magical fleece that Jason seeks on his quest. It is said to bring prosperity and power to its owner and is guarded by a dragon in the land of Colchis.

Hades: The god of the Underworld, ruler of the realm of the dead. He is the brother of Zeus and Poseidon and is married to Persephone.

Harpies: Winged creatures with the bodies of birds and the heads of women. They are known for stealing food and causing chaos.

Hercules: The greatest hero of Greek mythology, known for his incredible strength. He completed the famous Twelve Labors, which included tasks like defeating the Nemean Lion and capturing Cerberus.

Hydra: A multi-headed serpent defeated by Hercules as one of his Twelve Labors. When one head was cut off, two more grew back in its place.

Iolaus: Hercules's nephew who helped him defeat the Hydra by cauterizing the necks of the creature's heads to prevent them from growing back.

Ithaca: The island home of Odysseus. After the Trojan War, Odysseus embarks on a long journey to return to Ithaca and reunite with his family.

Jason: The hero who led the Argonauts on a quest to find the Golden Fleece. His adventures were filled with challenges, monsters, and the help of his companions.

Labyrinth: A giant maze built by Daedalus to house the Minotaur on the island of Crete. It is so complex that no one who enters can find their way out without help.

Medusa: A Gorgon with snakes for hair. Anyone who looks directly at her turns to stone. Perseus defeats her using a reflective shield to avoid her deadly gaze.

Minotaur: A creature with the body of a man and the head of a bull. It lived in the Labyrinth on Crete and was defeated by Theseus.

Medea: A powerful sorceress who helped Jason retrieve the Golden Fleece. She later became Jason's wife.

Nemean Lion: A lion with impenetrable skin that Hercules defeated as the first of his Twelve Labors. Hercules wore the lion's pelt as a symbol of his strength.

Odysseus: The clever hero of the **Odyssey**, known for his intelligence and resourcefulness. He faced many challenges on his journey home from the Trojan War, including the Cyclops, Sirens, and Scylla.

Orpheus: A legendary musician whose music could charm anything, even the gods of the Underworld. He attempted to rescue his wife, Eurydice, from the Underworld using the power of his music.

Persephone: The daughter of Demeter and the queen of the Underworld. She was abducted by Hades, and her story explains the changing of the seasons.

Polyphemus: A Cyclops and the son of Poseidon. He captures Odysseus and his men, but they escape by outsmarting him and blinding his single eye.

Poseidon: The god of the sea and brother of Zeus and Hades. He plays a key role in many Greek myths, especially those involving the ocean.

River Styx: A river that separates the world of the living from the Underworld. Souls must cross it to reach the land of the dead, and gods swear unbreakable oaths by it.

Sirens: Sea creatures whose beautiful singing lured sailors to their doom by causing them to crash their ships on the rocks. Odysseus famously resisted their song by having his men plug their ears with beeswax.

Theseus: A hero who defeated the Minotaur in the Labyrinth with the help of Ariadne. He is also known for many other adventures and acts of bravery.

Trojan War: A famous war between the Greeks and the city of Troy. Odysseus played a key role in the Greek victory with his idea of the Trojan Horse.

Underworld: The realm of the dead, ruled by Hades. It is where the souls of the deceased go after they die and is guarded by Cerberus.

Zeus: The king of the gods and ruler of the sky. He is the most powerful of the Olympian gods and plays a role in many Greek myths.

Conclusion

Congratulations, young adventurer! You've journeyed through the exciting world of **Greek mythology**, learning about daring heroes, fearsome monsters, powerful gods, and important life lessons along the way. But your adventure doesn't have to end here. The world of myths is filled with endless stories, and now it's your turn to continue exploring!

Create Your Own Myth

Now that you've learned so much about Greek myths, why not try creating your own? Imagine yourself as a hero embarking on a great quest—what challenges would you face? Who would your friends and companions be? What creatures or gods might you encounter along the way? You could even write your own story inspired by the myths we've explored in this book.

Maybe your adventure takes you to a mysterious island, where you must solve ancient riddles to find a hidden treasure. Or perhaps you meet a creature no one has ever seen before and must figure out how to defeat it or befriend it. The possibilities are endless!

Here are a few ideas to get you started:

- **A Quest for a Magical Artifact:** Like Jason's search for the Golden Fleece, your hero could be on a quest to find a powerful item. What is the artifact, and why is it so important?
- **A Battle Against a Monster:** Inspired by Perseus's defeat of Medusa or Theseus's battle with the Minotaur, your hero could face a terrifying creature. How will you defeat it?
- **A Journey to the Underworld:** Like Orpheus, your hero might need to journey into the Underworld to rescue someone they love. What challenges will you face along the way?

Share Your Stories

Greek myths were passed down through generations as exciting stories that people told each other. Now, you can do the same! Once you've created your own myth or adventure, share it with your friends, family, or even in a class project. You might be surprised at how many new ideas and stories come to life when you start talking about mythology.

Remember, mythology is all about using your imagination. Whether you're writing about gods, monsters, or magical lands, the most important thing is to have fun and let your creativity shine.

Keep Exploring

There's still so much more to discover in the world of Greek mythology. From famous heroes like **Achilles** to lesser-known gods and creatures, there are countless stories waiting to be uncovered. You can explore other myths from around the world too—Norse, Egyptian, and Roman myths are full of adventure and excitement just like the Greek ones!

So, what's next for you? Will you dive deeper into the myths of ancient Greece, or will you explore the legends of other cultures? No matter what path you choose, your own mythological journey has just begun.

Thank you for joining me on this epic adventure through Greek mythology! I hope these stories have inspired you to be brave, curious, and always ready for the next adventure. Now, it's time to go out and create your own legendary tales. Who knows? Maybe one day, your story will become a myth that others will tell for years to come.

Happy adventuring, young hero!

Made in the USA
Columbia, SC
24 October 2024